What women want men to MANSPLAIN

What women want men to MANSPLAIN
a quick reference guide

Published by Talisman,

An imprint of AMF Media Ltd, 2019

ISBN 978-1-9161181-4-0

WHAT WOMEN WANT MEN TO

MANSPLAIN

A QUICK REFERENCE GUIDE

What women want men to MANSPLAIN

What women want men to MANSPLAIN

What women want men to MANSPLAIN

What women want men to MANSPLAIN

What women want men to MANSPLAIN

What women want men to MANSPLAIN

What women want men to MANSPLAIN

What women want men to MANSPLAIN

What women want men to MANSPLAIN

What women want men to MANSPLAIN

What women want men to MANSPLAIN

What women want men to MANSPLAIN

What women want men to MANSPLAIN

What women want men to MANSPLAIN

What women want men to MANSPLAIN

What women want men to MANSPLAIN

What women want men to MANSPLAIN

What women want men to MANSPLAIN

What women want men to MANSPLAIN

What women want men to MANSPLAIN

What women want men to MANSPLAIN

What women want men to MANSPLAIN

What women want men to MANSPLAIN

What women want men to MANSPLAIN

What women want men to MANSPLAIN

What women want men to MANSPLAIN

What women want men to MANSPLAIN

What women want men to MANSPLAIN

What women want men to MANSPLAIN

What women want men to MANSPLAIN

What women want men to MANSPLAIN

What women want men to MANSPLAIN

What women want men to MANSPLAIN

What women want men to MANSPLAIN

What women want men to MANSPLAIN

What women want men to MANSPLAIN

What women want men to MANSPLAIN

What women want men to MANSPLAIN

What women want men to MANSPLAIN

What women want men to MANSPLAIN

What women want men to MANSPLAIN

What women want men to MANSPLAIN

What women want men to MANSPLAIN

What women want men to MANSPLAIN

What women want men to MANSPLAIN

What women want men to MANSPLAIN

What women want men to MANSPLAIN

What women want men to MANSPLAIN

What women want men to MANSPLAIN

What women want men to MANSPLAIN

What women want men to MANSPLAIN

What women want men to MANSPLAIN

What women want men to MANSPLAIN

What women want men to MANSPLAIN

What women want men to MANSPLAIN

What women want men to MANSPLAIN

What women want men to MANSPLAIN

What women want men to MANSPLAIN

What women want men to MANSPLAIN

What women want men to MANSPLAIN

What women want men to MANSPLAIN

What women want men to MANSPLAIN

What women want men to MANSPLAIN

What women want men to MANSPLAIN

What women want men to MANSPLAIN

What women want men to MANSPLAIN

What women want men to MANSPLAIN

What women want men to MANSPLAIN

What women want men to MANSPLAIN

What women want men to MANSPLAIN

What women want men to MANSPLAIN

What women want men to MANSPLAIN

What women want men to MANSPLAIN

What women want men to MANSPLAIN

What women want men to MANSPLAIN

What women want men to MANSPLAIN

What women want men to MANSPLAIN

What women want men to MANSPLAIN

What women want men to MANSPLAIN

What women want men to MANSPLAIN

What women want men to MANSPLAIN

What women want men to MANSPLAIN

What women want men to MANSPLAIN

What women want men to MANSPLAIN

What women want men to MANSPLAIN

What women want men to MANSPLAIN

What women want men to MANSPLAIN

What women want men to MANSPLAIN

What women want men to MANSPLAIN

What women want men to MANSPLAIN

What women want men to MANSPLAIN

What women want men to MANSPLAIN

What women want men to MANSPLAIN

What women want men to MANSPLAIN

What women want men to MANSPLAIN

What women want men to MANSPLAIN

What women want men to MANSPLAIN

www.ingramcontent.com/pod-product-compliance
Lightning Source LLC
Chambersburg PA
CBHW080521030726
47592CB00012B/3431

* 9 7 8 1 9 1 6 1 1 8 1 4 0 *